# Where We Worship

# Sikh
# Gurdwara

Kanwaljit Kaur-Singh

## W
# FRANKLIN WATTS
### NEW YORK • LONDON • SYDNEY

This is the khanga symbol that is used
to represent the Sikh faith.

For Simran Singh

© 1998 Franklin Watts
96 Leonard Street
London
EC2A 4RH

Franklin Watts Australia
14 Mars Road
Lane Cove
NSW 2066

ISBN 0 7496 3155 4

Dewey Decimal Classification Number 294.6

A CIP Catalogue record for this book is available from
the British Library

**Editor:** Samantha Armstrong
**Series Designer:** Kirstie Billingham
**Illustrator:** Gemini Patel
**Religious Education Consultant:** Margaret Barratt, M.A. Religious Education lecturer and author
**Sikh Consultant:** Indarjit Singh OBE, Director of Network of Sikh Organisations
**Reading Consultant:** Prue Goodwin, Reading and Language Information Centre, Reading

Printed in Hong Kong

# Contents

# Gurdwaras around the world

A **gurdwara** is a place where Sikhs meet to worship God. There are gurdwaras all around the world. A gurdwara can be a room in a Sikh home.

# Sikh belief

Sikhs believe in one God who was not born and will not die. He is everywhere all the time. They believe that God created all of us so that everyone is **equal.** The **Ik Onkar** sign means that there is only one God.

This is the Ik Onkar sign. ▷

◁ This gurdwara is in India.

7

# The Gurus

A man called **Guru Nanak** started the Sikh religion in an area of India called **Punjab.** Nine other Gurus followed and taught Guru Nanak's teachings. **'Guru'** means wise teacher in the **Punjabi** language.

△ There are often pictures of the Gurus in gurdwaras. Here Guru Nanak is shown with the nine Gurus seated on mats around him.

# Outside a gurdwara

Outside every gurdwara flies a flag called the **Nishan Sahib**. In the middle of it is the **khanda** symbol. This shows a sword that is sharp on both sides, a circle and two more swords. The circle means that God is always present. The swords remind Sikhs to stand up for truth and to help those in need.

◀ The Nishan Sahib is triangular and is an orangey colour called saffron.

# Inside a gurdwara

A gurdwara has a big hall which is used for worship. The special Sikh book, the **Guru Granth Sahib** is kept in the hall. There is also a kitchen and a dining room called a **langar hall**.

The Guru ▷
Granth Sahib
is written in
the Sikh
language,
Punjabi.

The Guru Granth Sahib was written by the Gurus. In it are hymns called **shabads**. They teach Sikhs about God and how to love and serve all God's people. A **chauri** is waved over the book to protect it.

# Guru Granth Sahib

The Guru Granth Sahib rests on cushions on a platform in the gurdwara, with a canopy over it. When it is closed it is covered in beautiful cloths called **rumalas**. At the end of the day it is put away carefully.

The Guru Granth Sahib ▷ is covered with rumalas when no-one is reading it.

# Showing respect

When Sikhs enter a gurdwara, they take off their shoes and cover their heads. They bow or kneel in front of the Guru Granth Sahib to show their **respect** for the Gurus' teachings.

◀ These Sikh children are kneeling and bowing so that their foreheads touch the ground.

# Making an offering

Offerings of food or money are left in the gurdwara.
They are used for people who need help.

◁ The children
put money into a
collection box.

# Worship in a gurdwara

To worship in a gurdwara everyone sits on the floor in front of the Guru Granth Sahib. The people at the **service** are called the congregation or **sangat.**

Men and women usually sit on opposite sides of the hall. In some gurdwaras everyone sits together.

Here the men and women are ▷ sitting separately but this does not always happen.

# A service

During a service, the Guru Granth Sahib is read in **Punjabi**. Sometimes the reading is done by the **granthi** who works at the gurdwara. He explains the reading and tells stories about the Gurus' lives.

Before Guru Nanak's time, women were treated badly in India. They were not allowed to worship with men. Guru Nanak taught that men and women are equal.

A Sikh woman is reading one ▷ of the shabads or holy songs. She turns the pages of the book very carefully.

# Singing in a service

During the service the shabads from the Guru Granth Sahib are sung by singers called **ragis**. The ragis play the harmonium and Indian drums called **tabla**.

# Karah Prashad

At the end of a service everyone eats a sweet called the **Karah Prashad**. Eating it together reminds Sikhs that all people are equal.

▽ Karah Prashad is a sweet paste made from sugar, butter, flour and water.

21

Afterwards everybody eats together in the langar hall. The food is called **langar**.

△ The food is vegetarian, never meat, so that everyone can enjoy some.

◁ The langar is cooked and served by both men and women. This shows that Sikh men and women share looking after the family and doing the housework.

22

# The five 'k's

Some Sikhs wear five special Sikh things. Each one begins with the letter 'k' so they are called the five 'k's. They were first started by the tenth Guru, Guru Gobind Singh.

Kesh means hair. Many Sikhs do not cut their hair. This is so that they are just as God made them.

A Kara is a steel bracelet that reminds Sikhs of God and to do good deeds for him.

Kacchera are shorts worn under a Sikh's clothes to show goodness and action.

The Kirpan is a sword with which to stand up for what is right.

The Kanga is a small wooden comb that Sikhs carry as a sign of cleanliness.

# Sikh dress

All Sikhs must keep their hair tidy and cover it at the gurdwara. Sikh men and boys often wear **turbans** or **patkas** to cover their uncut hair. Sikh women wear a long scarf called a **chunni**.

Young boys can ▶ cover their hair under a patka which is like a small turban.

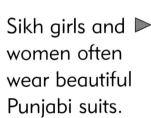

Sikh girls and ▶ women often wear beautiful Punjabi suits.

# School in a gurdwara

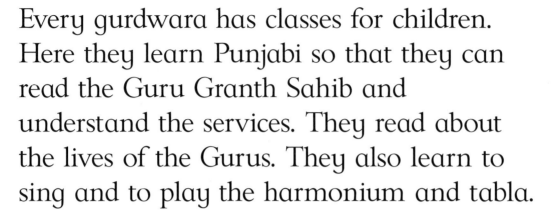

Every gurdwara has classes for children. Here they learn Punjabi so that they can read the Guru Granth Sahib and understand the services. They read about the lives of the Gurus. They also learn to sing and to play the harmonium and tabla.

Children also help around the gurdwara. This is called **sewa** which means helping others. By doing this children learn the Sikh way of life.

# Glossary

| | |
|---|---|
| **chauri** | a whisk that is waved over the Guru Granth Sahib |
| **chunni** | a long scarf worn by Sikh women to cover their heads in a gurdwara |
| **equal** | in the Sikh religion, people are equal to each other and everybody enjoys the same love and respect |
| **granthi** | a reader of the Guru Granth Sahib who leads services |
| **gurdwara** | a place of worship for Sikhs |
| **guru** | a wise teacher |
| **Guru Granth Sahib** | the Sikh holy book |
| **Guru Nanak** | the man who started the Sikh religion. He is the first Sikh Guru |
| **harmonium** | Indian musical instrument with a keyboard |
| **Ik Onkar** | the Sikh sign that means there is only one God |
| **Karah Prashad** | a sweet that is shared at the end of a service to show that everyone is equal |
| **khanda** | the sign on the Sikh flag |
| **langar** | the food that is eaten by everyone after a service |

| | |
|---|---|
| **langar hall** | a room in a gurdwara where everyone gathers to eat after a service |
| **Nishan Sahib** | the Sikh flag that flies outside gurdwaras and other Sikh buildings |
| **patka** | the piece of material worn by Sikh boys to cover their uncut hair |
| **Punjab** | the area of India where the Sikh way of worship started |
| **Punjabi** | the language spoken in Punjab |
| **ragis** | Sikh musicians who sing shabads from the Guru Granth Sahib |
| **respect** | to treat well |
| **rumalas** | cloths used to cover the Guru Granth Sahib |
| **sangat** | a gathering of Sikhs in a service |
| **shabads** | hymns from the Guru Granth Sahib |
| **service** | a meeting of Sikhs in a gurdwara |
| **sewa** | helping others |
| **tabla** | drums that come from India |
| **turban** | the piece of material worn by Sikh men to cover their uncut hair |

# Index

**Photographic acknowledgements:**
**Cover:** Ann and Bury Peerless, Steve Shott Photography.
P6 Ann and Bury Peerless
P7 Sikh Messenger Publications

P8 Ann and Bury Peerless
P9 Carlos Reyes-Manzo, Andes Press Agency
P17 Carlos Reyes-Manzo, Andes Press Agency

All other photographs are by Steve Shott Photography.

With thanks to Khalsa Jatha, Shepherd's Bush Gurdwara.